Animals

Animals

Prose poems on sentiency decency and indecency by

Anita Nahal

© 2025 Anita Nahal. All rights reserved.
This material may not be reproduced in any form, published,
reprinted, recorded, performed, broadcast,
rewritten, or redistributed without
the explicit permission of Anita Nahal.
All such actions are strictly prohibited by law.

Cover design by Shay Culligan
Cover image by cottonbro on Pexels
Author photo by Anita Nahal

ISBN: 978-1-63980-738-3
Library of Congress Control Number: 2025937900

Kelsay Books
502 South 1040 East, A-119
American Fork, Utah 84003
Kelsaybooks.com

for all

Acknowledgments

Some of these poems have been previously published or are forthcoming. The author tends to revise her poems long after acceptance and publication. Therefore, some of the previously published ones reappear in a slightly different avatar in this book.

The Cathexis-Northwest-Press: "Would you like to die in another's trash?"

Citiscapes Anthology: "Zoos," "Vehicular fragmentation," "Leaving me"

The Ekphrastic Review: "Whom shall I blame or groom," "Singing flowers and whales," "The Kongo Nkisi Nkondi and the riding dog"

Hey . . . Spilt milk is spilt, nothing else: "You, me, and the animals"

The Journal of Expressive Writing: "Races"

Kisses at the espresso bar (Kelsay Books, 2022): "Koala and Judases," "Humans and extinctions"

The Mackinaw Journal: "Mulesing," "Animals do not plan for war," "Please don't foster me," "Chains," "Nameless stray dogs"

The Mountain Was Abuzz Anthology: "The story of the endangered Himalayan respect"

The Old Rat Journal: "A pigeon's sound soothes"

Pen-in-Hand: "A bear on 365," "Wolf," "Decapods will rebel one day," "Survival of the fittest," "If my pack is good, I'm good," "Memory"

Rasoi (Kitchen) Anthology (Forthcoming): "Good children, good dogs," "Sweet tooth remembrances"

Relics Anthology (Forthcoming): "Unpartnered relics"

Setu: "Gandhi, Gus and anew"
What's wrong with us Kali women? (Kelsay Books, 2021): "It's not all about sex," "Family blood"
Women and Cities Anthology (Forthcoming): "Running in tortured big cities," "A single mother in a city"

Contents

Introduction	15
You, me, and the animals	19
Decapods will rebel one day	20
Wolf	21
Good children and good dogs	22
Mulesing	23
Animals do not plan for war	24
Family blood	25
Gandhi, Gus, and anew	26
Running in tortured big cities	27
Races	28
A single mother in a city	29
Please don't foster me	30
If my pack is good, I'm good	31
Memory	32
It's not all about sex	33
Vehicular fragmentation and holy cow-hood	34
Koala and Judases	35
Safari	36
Would you like to die in another's trash?	37
Humans and extinctions	38
Underwater cages	39
A pigeon's sound soothes	40
Whom shall I blame or groom?	41
Elephant tusks	42
Sweet, sweet, sweet tooth	43
Experimentations	44
Chains	45
Singing flowers and whales	46
Survival of the fittest or sheer inconvenience	47
Zoos	48

Unpartnered relics	49
The story of the endangered Himalayan respect	50
The Kongo *Nkisi Nkondi* and the riding dog	51
Sadism	52
A bear on 395	53
Circus of life	54
Angoras, downs, alligators, snakes, cows, buffalos, rabbits, sheep, ostriches, etc., etc., etc.	55
Bullfight	56
Blood bank	57
Nameless stray dogs	58
Leaving me	59
Ride me if you must	60

Introduction

This poetry collection does not advocate against, or in favor of, meat eating. That is a personal choice. This collection emerges from a deep-seated disappointment in the way animals are treated by some people. The human race calls itself sentient, one that can perceive and feel. Yet, in some individuals, there seems to be an abysmal dearth of empathy, sentiments, or any modicum of regard for another living being.

Many times, we say, that this or that person behaves like an animal—I think we need to move away from that paradigm because animals certainly do not behave like some humans in pre-planned actions of mercilessness. And to deny that animals have feelings and sensitivities such as delight, pleasure, and pain reveals a deficiency in human perception at the way our world operates.

Numerous writers, leaders, thinkers, philosophers, scientists, and others have spoken against the heartlessness of some human behavior towards animals. George Bernard Shaw said, "Man's inhumanity to man is only surpassed by his cruelty to animals." Immanuel Kant said, "We can judge the heart of a man by his treatment of animals." And Mahatma Gandhi said, "There is little that separates humans from other sentient beings. We all feel joy; we all crave to be alive and to live freely, and we all share this planet together."[1]

The poems in this short collection seek to draw attention to the inhumane activities to which animals are sometimes subjected by addressing some of the major issues of global animal rights, such

---

[1] All quotes are from: *Animal matters* (no date) *Animal Matters*. Available at: www.animalmatters.org/quotes/general/#:~:text=%E2%80%9CMan's%20inhumanity%20to%20man%20is,by%20his%20cruelty%20to%20animals.%E2%80%9D&text=%E2%80%9CIf%20a%20man%20aspires%20towards,is%20from%20injury%20to%20animals.%E2%80%9D (Accessed: 18 April 2025).

as general neglect and cruelty, animal testing, animals in sports, hunting, and races, animal abandonment, animals in fashion, animals in the blood bank, encroachment of animals lands, ivory trade, pollution of waters and forests, to name a few. Woven into some of the poems is also human abuse towards other humans that animals might observe and in turn display love and patience.

Herein lies the essence of my poems: to remind us that all living beings are sentient. The only difference is that animals cannot express in a language we understand. The look in their eyes, their shudders, their running away from us, the hiding, the barking, and even wounding us are all their ways of telling us to leave them alone. Live and let live in peace. Ethics and morality remind us that there are certain universal truths in the way the cosmos functions. Subjecting any living being to any kind of abject malice goes against the generally acceptable ethical grain.

My attachment to the environment and the non-human species on our planet is close to my heart. Ever since I was a young child, I would observe the mistreatment of animals and of our planet. I have written a number of ecopoems previously as well, a few of which are reproduced in this volume. Collectively, this volume is a nod of veneration to living beings that exist in the circle of life.

As I conclude, I begin my appreciation and thanks with my son for his unconditional love, support, and encouragement. He is my closest friend and a blessing to me.

I thank Kelsay Books for believing in me and offering *Animals* a warm space in their publishing house.

I also thank the readers of my poems for their interest in prose poetry, a style in which I mostly write. In some ways, it's akin to Beat poetry and Spoken word, though there are distinct variables of difference with both.

Finally, a huge thank you and gratitude to the animals with whom we reside in this world.

~Anita Nahal~

You, me, and the animals

Many worlds in one, for you, me, and them. Our living edifices might be different, and a reasoning mind is supposed to help, yet outside and inside filth, disrespect, blame, and insult define decency and indecency—compatible bed partners for some. The pendulum shakes its unkept head as thinking minds are at a loss and lost. And the stiff, coiffured sentiency becomes a catchphrase for the arrogant. We crib. We complain. Eternal narcissists, we blow steam recklessly, continuously, like rickety engines, like leaking pressure cookers, like conscious flatulence. They seem to know more, and we look down upon them. Who really are the animals? Do we even want that word in dictionaries anymore? Beasts, brutes, and creatures are synonyms filled to the dirtiest rims of conscious limbs. Who really are we and them? Who are the animals?

Decapods will rebel one day

In oceans, in nets, in receptacles, in boiling water, in mouths. One day. Tempting many passersby at a restaurant window stood a glass container full to the top. Full of crabs, lobsters in some kind of slimy water, being prepared for the scalding burns and then the chop. Water is perhaps rarely changed. Wasn't any need when death by murder awaited them in a world deranged. Sherlock Holmes, come quick! Look for the clues, shake my blues, let the decapods go; they've paid their dues. My long sigh fogged the winter pane when a gloved hand picked one crab and one lobster, tossing them carelessly, pitilessly, hastily into large pots of boiling water. I could hear from the butcher no gasp, no stutter. And as I walked away, crestfallen, struggling with big words like humanity, immortality, and sentient empathy, I looked back, and the crustaceans, so-called non-sentients, fluttered around as they sank, writhing from agony that some would have us believe they don't feel. I could possibly swear I saw their red, swollen eyes open and watching, with their one stalk each pointing straight up, shaking right to left, repeatedly. Like an admonishment. Karma is not cloaked, nor is it like Rip Van Winkle. Hollywood displays advanced aliens looking like decapods. Guilt? Fear? One day.

Wolf

And then there was a nondescript news item that became big in a few hours. An innocent young wolf with a tight muzzle was photographed. Photographed just before. Just before it was shot between the eyes. Like it was a dirty wooden board for practicing bullseye. Like it was an old hunk of metal for training rounds. And so, grow the infested sports mounds. Resigned and despondent, looking down, not at the camera, yet regal in its last moments, shy, hushed, it knew its fate. And nearby, hurriedly gathered the rodents. The victory grins on them, eager proponents. After the shot, it lay limp, glorious in death, reflecting mucky, wasted human thoughts and actions. Of human anger, pride, and power. Superiority and egotistical homo sapiens make a heady, intoxicating mix. Laughter and elbow nudges resounded well into and onto nocturnal waves. And the young wolf became the winds that blow over the hills, the rustle of the evening dried leaves, the reminiscences of its footprints in the mud, the eternal, endless waiting heartbeats of its pack.

Good children and good dogs

Angrily, he throws the faintly overcooked rice on the floor with a swirl of his wrist. Second time around, he hurls the bowl of slightly undercooked rice at the wall with a spin of his wrist. So many humans and animals, hungry or not, would not. Both times the steel containers fall and twirl noisily like unhinged spinning tops before resting near his feet. He looks at her quizzically. Eyes fixed unflinchingly. Trembling, she lowers her gaze, raking her mind, not sure how to cook to perfection. The child eats the first cooked rice, asking for more. The dog laps up his given rice, wagging his tail for more. She cooks it a third time. It passes the test. *See, if I hadn't thrown the first two bowls of rice, how'd you have learned to make it to perfection?* His mouth, now full of flawlessly prepared starch, mixes with ego and narcissism, snickering, jumbling around like street marbles in a rusting trash can. The wife gives an air kiss between tears to the child, pats the dog, cleans the smeared walls and floor. Her *rasoi* had been a battleground. She an unwilling soldier.

Rasoi: Hindi word for kitchen

Mulesing

The other day, in a video, a nightmare came to life. I wanted to watch. To think. To feel. To see my kind sink beyond comprehension. A terrified sheep cried. Flayed its head and legs. Struggled to be free. Like a fish in a net. Or a person being bullied. Being brutalized. Isn't fright the same for the sheep, fish, them, you, and me? Eyes wide open in shock, the sheep continues wriggling. Much smaller than the person mulesing it. Bruising it. At their mercy. Deemed of a decent life unworthy. Yelps went not just unheard. Not just unpacified. Tactics not just unchanged. Executioner style, the sheep is hurled against the wall. As if from the end of a dirty nail, a splinter is flicked. As if from the tip of a finger, a fly from a drink is scooped and slinged. No matter, the sheep had eyes staring and breath blowing towards the person. Sounds followed, of striking the wall—smashing, splitting, breaking, and a shriek. It fell limp and dead. End of life and torment. Now you can profit-mules it. Later, have a feast of the slaughterers. You wear your Merino proudly. And I see an exhaust fan letting out the stench of your malice, which will reek for centuries like *Odense* repurposed toilet barrels.

**Odense:* On the evacuation of 14th-century toilets in Odense, archeologists found repurposed toilet barrels still stinking of poop.

This poem is inspired by the practice of mulesing, where portions of a sheep's skin and flesh near the tail area are cut off while the animals are alive. Mulesing is legal in some countries where Merino wool sheep are mulesed to ensure the quality of the wool remains uninfected by fly or larvae breeding under the layers of their skin.

Animals do not plan for war

And tear apart. Or just tear. Sometimes insects can tear other insects. Reflex. Defense. Sometimes, chimpanzees move deep into another territory. Kill a male. Or wipe out another group. Like the *Gombe*. Sometimes whales or other amphibians, or some mammals like lions, may devour their own young. It's quick. It's sudden. It's bloody. It's instinctive. Sounds gruesome, like ancient mindless acts of ordeal repeated because history repeats itself. Yet no real planning. No copious copies of paperwork. No spreadsheets projecting actions and reactions. No outlining maps with routes. No date fixing. No time matching. No suited-booted standing in impenetrable war rooms. No devious hearts preconceiving the end-of-life fluids gone up in fumes. They don't have Homo Sapien haughtiness, or, as some say, smartness. I see clear sands with only red hands walking their way into civilizations. Yours, yours, and yours. Clashes that lead to no bounteous dashes. No respites. Not even respecting ancient rules of not fighting after sundown.

Gombe chimpanzee: Documented research by Jane Goodall has revealed that groups of Gombe chimpanzee located in the Kigoma region, Tanzania, indulged in a four-year war for territorial rights between 1974 and 1978.

Family blood

As I drove down Route X earlier than six a.m., on the side, not where my car was, lay a white sheet protruding upwards. By itself. Stationery, forlorn, unclaimed. Flashing police cars raced by. My heart palpitated fast. It seemed all the cars on my side were slowing, gliding, perhaps wondering why a blank, bulging cloth lay solitary. By itself. Had no one yet in this baffling, maddening, desolate world said, *That's my own!* For now, just the road to it lay claim. Without the dueling squabble of blame. At first, I anticipated it was a poor deer. Poor deer. Poor, poor deer, not thinking about the poor, poor deer's family. But a blocked highway for miles could not be for an animal, right? Where was the damaged car? Or cars? Other people? Ambulance? I wasn't sure for whom my prayers were, human or deer. Hurt inside was grave as the protruding white sheet seemed dismissed, like I had done a deer, simply calling it poor. And then, humans scorn even their living.

Gandhi, Gus, and anew

Everywhere, there's a weird artificial jungle. Under, around, skirting tween, and on our physiques too that are naked and weeping. Sirens screech. People scream. Things thud, clump, jingle, roam, romp, and mingle. And destinies go in a loop. Loop. Loop. Watching from the clouds, Gandhi comes visiting. From somewhere, Kaa could be heard singing, *Do you know I can eat in one gulp your khadi cloth, you, and all? Smug about your Ahimsa, eh? One simple morsel, that's all it will take. To have you in my tummy bake. You, your khadi cloth, and all.* Gandhi retorted, *You don't have enough might to eat me. My Ahimsa will give you diarrhea.* Baloo chuckled, sighed, in his deep baritone: *And there you have it, Gandhi. Kaa is crazy, crazy, crazy tizzy. To eat you and pretend he's satisfied, busy, bright, blaring, and glitzy. And there you have it, Gandhi. Kaa's crazy, crazy, crazy, tizzy.* Sher Khan roars, Bagheera laughs with Mowgli on his back. And Gandhi runs towards a light. Under a tiny tent sat *Gus* with a torch, shivering, ears upright. Shadows loom. Loom. Loom. Of Gandhi, Martin, Mandela. And all our ancestors. And all the souls who died peacefully or tragically. Gus barely lifts the tent, and Gandhi's tears fall on his deer-like nose and onto the parched Earth below. A new leaf is soon seen *blowin' in the wind.*

**Khadi:* Hand-spun natural cloth

**Ahimsa:* Nonviolence

**Blowin' in the Wind* is a song written by Bob Dylan in 1962.

This poem is inspired by a 2021 American Netflix drama series, *Sweet Tooth*. In it, hybrids of humans and animals attempt to save themselves from pure humans. Gus is the main character. The poem is also inspired by *The Jungle Book* movie.

Running in tortured big cities

Sometimes, some places can become a never-healing wound. Band-aids in their guile drowned. Festering on top of natural times gone. No lessons drawn. Like big cities with tortured histories. With more than one traumatic narrative. With hundreds of souls roaming aimlessly like pets left behind in war zones. Clones with no mass, blood, or bones. Not needed anymore. Not wanted anymore. Pets would not leave humans behind. Wouldn't have resigned. Some cities eat themselves from the inside like termites to wood and still not be gratified. Termites are blind yet eusocial, and generations co-exist. Don't go wild like humans chewing, chomping, chewing, chomping, emptying the nucleus for all to ogle. Like useless men running towards rape. Like the homeless fending for themselves. Like the careless leaving live cigarettes behind. Like thieves out to loot. Or the uncontrollable gunning around. Or the unattended crying in the pound. Everyone is adrift seeking some precious ways to feel normal. Normal, normal, please, I beseech, no more, no more abnormal. Even cougar P-22 pleaded. Empty was his heart, human maligned, alone without one of his kind. We need to be like the few remaining animals. Just eating, playing, grooming, and sleeping without sentient torture.

This poem is inspired by the cougar named P-22, who roamed the limited green areas of Los Angeles in search of a mate. Authorities built a fully ecological wildlife bridge over a six-lane highway so it could cross over to the jungle on the other side and find a mate. P-22 died before the bridge was completed.

Races

I call my hair wild when it's not set. That's the way I like it. Right down to each curl's rotating bit. I fret and fume that I'm looking horrible. Even when blow-dried, nothing seems restorable. How a small thing as wildness in hair, attitude, and running unbound is a privilege for many. Not for all. Not for the disabled. Or the sick. Or in modern slavery. Or in personal bondage. Nor for the jockeys and little children and Capuchin monkeys. Nor is it for horses, dogs, camels, cocks, and other defenseless in so-called grand, global games. It is a designed mess. Controlled and detailed are their places and paces in unnecessary races. Such is the fad. Pushed, prodded, some separated from their mothers too soon, whipped and euthanized because they were not advantageous enough. Or your ill treatment did them in. And then, at their dough losses, the handlers have the gall to huff and puff. Spectators are mostly mute. Such is the tempting strength of the moolah glue. What is it that slides some humans into the crooked fringe? Injected with some frenzied syringe. Without a thought, limp, used figures become mocked carcasses. Many wronged breaths leave, become energy all around for us to feel or repel. The roars, the hollers, the sticks, the whips, the money pulls, the bets won and wasted. Who is going to calculate the morality cost?

This poem is inspired by the use of many animals in races or fights. Little children are also used in camel races. Currently, in some camel races, automated robots are used.

A single mother in a city

Tries not to falter. Too many admonishers. Too many tricking tarnishers. Not in the animal world. Only small-large predators hunting for survival. Human predators hunt for greed, jealousy, power, sick abuse. There's a certain amount of continuous, competitive reprisal. I think I'll go play, learn, and dance with single animal moms. Build a nest high up in the flowing branches, like orangutan moms. Or regurgitate food eaten days before to feed my young like penguin moms. I'll also hold hands with elephant moms and aunts and surround my young in a loving, saving embrace. I'll fill my belly with water and cool my young like least terns. And be a super single mom like a ruby-throated hummingbird. Or, like kangaroo moms, keep the pouch always cozy and secure. And like a lioness, cheetah, or bear, there's nothing I wouldn't do to protect my child. I could also meander slowly along life's path, like sloth moms. And lick and clean like dog moms. I can't bring my single animal mom-friends to a city where poachers and hunters sit at the overpriced gates of a crumbling citadel. They wouldn't be able to build, dwell, or illumine. They wouldn't last like I did, continuously trained to be familiar with conniving humans.

Please don't foster me

If you don't really love me. There I was among countless canines, baffled, homeless, deprived, disenfranchised, like votes in poor neighborhoods. Too many foster children in the care of the uncaring. Like countless moons waxing, wanning, old or new, bumping against each other in a sky bereft of space. Unfeeling, cold profit hoarding. Some friends lay lifeless, some eyeless, all clueless. I couldn't find my mom or dad. Or siblings. So many litters littered. Connections, remembrances forgotten. I don't even get my daily morsels. Those few bits and pieces for surviving, hardly thriving. Thrown on dirty floors, no containers, while you seek donations for self-expansion. Winters, summers, or rains—the outdoors is where I'm deposited, like a piece of mail meant for someone else. Like I was born in the wild to nurture myself. I'm chained sometimes too, and I cry for freedom, some side legroom, some quiet time for myself. Even my cousins in the wild don't lie in their own bodily release.

This poem is inspired by news reports of dog foster homes that mistreat their four-legged residents.

If my pack is good, I'm good

My motherly heart swells like a birthday balloon. It's also embarrassed. Am not over the moon doing my business in front of her. What would she make of the noises? Or my cleaning? Or the smells? Her pleading expectant eyes and one paw in the door persists. Insists. Like a stuck door latch key. Like nostalgic tea. I let her in and let go. If my pack is good, I am good. I nurture my pack with peanut butter and jam. Life is after all sugar and salt in one teaspoon. Partners, like balm and dry skin. Sometimes heat is high. Sometimes, low. Knead myself into a balanced dough. Her pleading eyes and one paw in the door persists. Insists. Like a stuck door latch key. Like nostalgic tea. I let her in and let go. If my pack is good, I'm good. Packs don't always need romance. That kind of love ain't in my destiny in this birth. I don't bother anymore. Don't dream it anymore. Seasons change, and I breathe in varying colors of leaves. Its bliss. Of my child and breathing itself. Memorabilia of life sprinkled with dried spilt milk lie on the mantelshelf. Her eyes and one paw in the door persists. Insists. Like a stuck door latch key. Like nostalgic tea. I let her in and let go. If my pack is good, I'm good.

This poem is inspired by research that tells us that dogs are pack animals; therefore, they follow us everywhere, including to the bathroom, so they can watch over us when we are vulnerable.

Memory

Tis a poem of letdowns and shutdowns. Of the brain cells in some, of humans in others. Of teaching chair yoga in nursing homes. To those in squeaky wheelchairs or fraying sofas who'd forget the *asanas* and me, easily. Whose afternoons and twilights are a mixed-up Rubik's cube. Confused, jumbled without a road map to walk back. Ain't nothing wrong with the system. It's fine. It's in place because it's required. It feeds, nurses, and changes the bedpan. It's a philosophy at war with itself. Of individualism. Of departing from home, being on one's own. *Go on, go find a job. Learn to be on your own.* Of growing up too soon or not to return ever. Of living with no more kids pestering those that spermed or wombed. Freedom of style, home, nakedness, and anytime sex anywhere in the house. Then karma comes full circle, and some are left with no familial warmth to douse flames of fears, depression, dementia, or Alzheimer's. Elephants age gracefully, like spring flowers into summer. A close-knit herd is like a winter pullover with just the right-tight stitches. The hardening of the hide, graying together, always recalling. The pride that builds from touching, releasing endorphins, not plaque buildup.

Asanas: Yoga poses

This poem is inspired by research that reveals elephants don't seem to develop Dementia or Alzheimer's because of their close social networks, due to which there is no amyloid plaque buildup, which is a cause of cognitive decline.

It's not all about sex

It was pretty dark, and the path was not lit except for the guide's powerful torch, which suddenly sprawled on treetops right in our path. We stood still, whispering, *What do you see? What do you see?* Hushing us, gesturing to follow him, and then hands in full stop. Right above us, a drama was ensuing. The sloths were not frightened by the glaring lights. The new mama, with the baby clinging to her breasts, was climbing fast. As fast as sloths in danger can. The stud sloth was in pursuit from another branch. His heat made him faster, and he reached right beneath the new mama, and then he retracted quite suddenly, knowing his heat wasn't going to be satisfied that day. After scratching himself thoroughly, he tried again. The baby sensed something and quite valiantly left his mama to stride up the branch alone. She pulled the baby back into her embrace. The stud knew it was only to be about consideration that day.

Vehicular fragmentation and holy cow-hood

You know how sometimes old folks are considered useless. And sit on benches outside elder homes, or their own, just people-watching, forced smiling, pretending busyness was their post-retirement job. Being cool even after a couple of ice cubes slid down their spine. Many old cows too sometimes can be found hunkering outside, pretending to be chillin, sleeping, blocking traffic in India. Horns go beeping, wheels go skirting, tirades go hurling, but they just lay munching. Their long, lush eyelashes flicker with simple acquiescence. Their fate planned. Like some passersby take it upon themselves to implant red *tilak* on their foreheads to guard their remaining, aging holiness. Forced sentiency is truant air down a trachea. Elder cows are left to roam the streets when they are beyond the age of milking. Like old people, they haven't left much to give others now. They aren't feeding but being fed now. Everyone's holy reverence stripped away. It's cold outside. It's always cold outside. There's something snug and familiar inside the four walls of nice homes. Bad homes can be cold, raw, painful, like cow leather skinned unflinchingly. Slayers are manifold and sometimes unmasked, like in *The Regime*. This is the elderly journey until someone runs them over. The huge bump and crunch and the yells that follow are silenced by people yammering, by piercing honks, by grinding dust, and sometimes just by thoughtless sentiency.

Tilak: Also known as Tika, is a mark on the forehead applied in quite a similar fashion as a bindi. Unlike in the case of bindi, which has no religious meaning, a tilak can signify sectarian affiliation.

The Regime: A 2024 limited HBO series starring Kate Winslet and Matthias Schoenaerts

Koala and Judases

Mean, mean people slowly unwrap like sundry skins. I welcomed them, so I hold culpability. They slither away, leaving me to create, tend, love, rear a new skin, over and over. Judases. The forest is desiccated, fragile. Perfect for a fire. I don't smoke. But I see your smoky tracks in my backyard, sore and fiery, leaving me to douse them with my own skin, my own fabrics, my own rush, over and over. Judases. Ghosts of the Amazonia, Derring Woods, Crooked Forest, the Tsingy, the Black Forest, the Tongass, the Sundarbans, and many more let out banshee screams often. See my bark, my leaves, my tiny legs heaped in layers on the sun's anchor. Judases. I see the residues from rampant wildfires spill just outside my abode. I see you and others cooking on those very dangerous embers. Judases. I don't watch. I observe. I look pointedly. That's my job. Like the Gods of all religions observing us. I may look short and cute, yet I thrive on tall eucalyptus that your pettiness can never reach, unless you burn the trees. I can live long except for your foolhardiness that lights a match or pulls along in old, smelly rags your infectious diseases. I'm forced to be your sins. Your self-absorption. Your juvenile behavior protruding like Pinocchio's nose. Judases.

Safari

So, you think you are God's gift on a safari? All tucked up in your fancy car, cameras ready, but wait! Who do you think is cast in the main role of a prepared shikari? No one. No one in life is safe, uncatchable, least of all the gait in your fate. You prowl around, fake-crowned and breathless, displaying your desires and fears all over the state. Did anyone tell you that nothing is clear; it's shadowy and bottomless. It's an illusion; just look beneath the magician's hat for the real bait. The unknown, maybe supreme sentients, watch us from somewhere high or beyond as you awkwardly use oxygen masks or binoculars to spot an exotic "non-sentient" under the sea or in the thick greens you think you have conned. But alas! It's a mirage; you aren't the divinely destined prescient.

Shikari: Hindi word for a hunter

This poem is inspired by news reports of tourists at safaris who do not adhere to rules and end up being mauled and killed.

Would you like to die in another's trash?

I see myself being sucked in. Gasping, pleading with the blare of mega ships drowning my hums and drones to notch it down. I'm slowly sinking like in quicksand. Unhurried descent, hard to extract. Like a leech, it will not stop. Careless human debris is evil hitchhiking in water life. Recklessness, heedlessness are foul human traits. Even among each other, some don't think how another could be affected by tons of body waste. Words, actions, viruses, feces, plastic, clothing, hair, nails, paper, bottles, furniture, attitude, anger, and negligence ingested and inside floating, grazing, gagging, filling stomachs, intestines, pulling appetites away. Confusing innocents in open, vast oceans, flowing rivers, silent lakes that their tummies are full. Their consumption stops. And then they sink or are washed ashore like irritant food particles stuck in teeth gaps spitted out in disgust occupying spaces just about anywhere. Would you like to die in the trash of amphibians? They don't collect their waste in pipes and dump it in waters. They don't sit around on beaches or have picnics and forget to clean up.

This poem is inspired by research about water pollution, including some that suggest that some about 800 species worldwide are affected by debris in the waters.

Humans and extinctions

The last hatchling of the ancient great roamer was born before humans came along to set ablaze antiquity. Ain't much left for a story. Boulders yawned with wide, open mouths. Let out ecstatic, climatic, high-pitched sounds. The skies were eerily discreet, with hands behind ears trying hard to decipher inaudible echoes that reverberated in the leaden, dreary, asafoetida-filled clouds. A kind of protracted, pungent, daunting humming could be heard miles away. Nothing could be kept at bay with downpours falling steady and demonstrative, descending into new rivers being charted at the confluence of liquids, heat, oxygen, mud. And *Pleistocene* in Australia lit up as tall-standing *Megalania* hit their chests, drumming the birth shower to an end as mom and fledgling watched the regalia reach its crescendo. The mom perched above the baby, completing the shedding of the amniotic fluid. She perched even higher above the cacophony. Anxious and vexed, ready to pounce and gobble any extinct predators emerging from abrasions in dimensions. Her eyesight acute, fully awake, observing the humans igniting the match. Dinosaurs vanished soon after. And friendships can be easily bought.

Pleistocene: Also referred to as the Ice Age

Ancient great roamer: Name given to the giant terrestrial lizard, Megalania, by Richard Owen, who first wrote about them

Underwater cages

Whose adrenaline is gushing and rushing like in ruthless drains? Blaring in echoless tunnels without gains. You. Who is underwater twirling in a machine on all fours? You. Who is full in the head with microdot beans and ripping the seams of their threadbare jeans? You. Whose hands are on a contraption to capture the exact moment a shark hurts its mouth trying to get food from a sturdy iron cage? You. You. Not the shark who is swimming around like a lark while you house yourself in the cage wanting to trip it! Have you checked your arrogance riding high nigh on your rage? This intense drama is on with you at center stage. Who gives a victory sign through oxygen devices when the shark struggles again and again with mega thrills as the aim? You. Who gives a silent, full-throated chuckle at having duped a famished so-called non-sentient in deep waters? You. Encroaching squatters. You. I see you pounding, vaulting in the cage, swinging your arms, *Mirror, mirror, on the wall, who is now the strongest of 'em all?* Delusional you and your mirror. Waiting to share on social media your shady haul. Even the shark wises up and loses interest. Nah, it shakes its fins in a rejecting wave, so-called sentient meat is not that palatable!

A pigeon's sound soothes

It's rare to hear a pigeon early morning in America. Just outside the door. Just outside the window. Somewhere outside. A very understated call in the dawn quietude. Not a wake-up siren. More like little children in school hesitant to say, present, yet do so fearing they'd be marked absent. It's rare to hear a pigeon early morning in America. Just outside the door. Just outside the window. Somewhere outside. Perhaps on the balcony ledge. Perhaps on the roof. Perhaps I am hallucinating. Perhaps I am hoping. I peer outside from all angles, yet the pigeon I don't see. City noises are beginning to awake and muffle its euphonious sounds. Sounds that unravel some memories. Not that I want to go back. Not that the same pigeons will greet me. Not that my parents are still there. Heck, I am even mortified of birds, you see! It's just that sounds of a pigeon unravel some memories. And I don't mind some nostalgia now and then.

Whom shall I blame or groom?

I'm cleaned and prepped and glistening in the looking glass. Lying in heavily scented, oiled-soiled palms like stolen gold coins, ready to play dirty. In beds or casinos. My disrespect is not sanctioned by Gods. So, whom shall I blame for breakage, confusion, pain-leaving, damp stain? Or whom shall I groom for luck, rethinking, piety, improved-swapped mentality? Or whom shall I groom in wonderous faith? Humans? Animals? Animals may not seek mirrors, glass, or gold. And the callous don't see them; they just destroy. And court jesters are punished, ridiculed, never to be set free. Hundreds of bees in the bonnet, or are there many bonnets on one bee? Roads are blocked. Passages gloated. Brains are lard-clogged. I hang my coat on the stand. Throw open the tight, molding windows. Watch the queen on the throne. Watch the starved men drool and prepare for antics. Watch nature mingle with my thoughts, my fears, my smiles, and my promises, like nervous pregnant mothers, human or animal, just before delivery. Ah, what a quagmire of semantics! Whom shall I blame, and whom shall I groom?

Elephant tusks

Are in decline. Trophy chasers reverberate with anger. No need to pamper. They are failing like drowned causes. And because humans can think, some don't. Hyperbolic, I'd say. Shakespeare, we need some fresh oxymorons. Less morons. And Rousseau, your "general will" could be imperfect. Most folks live in fanciful, deranged dreams. Perfection is perhaps paradise, like an evening walk on moonbeams. Not needed, really. For humans will stagnate, become boring. Like ChatGPT or robots, impeccably, fiercely structured. No organic mind or heart. Scarier, even more controlling, replacing human species in a false flow chart. Humans will adapt. As did elephants, birthing calves without tusks. Grasping for survival at the cusps. Scampering during the major flux at the crux of civil wars, external wars, or just hunting. Evolution doesn't take long. Humans can go take a hike. Far away, where no one will hear the spike in their strike. With their eyes reversed, they can watch their own puny teeth pulled to make ornaments, table decorations, and whatnot, satiating another species' voracious craving for the mysterious and the rare. Will be to the bones bare. It's a ferocious human peculiarity. You know—to grab, kill, and sell off cadavers, even of their own kind. Complex barbarity. Two to three sizes smaller than the elephant brain, it still claims primata in an unbreakable piñata.

This poem is inspired by statistics that reveal almost 20,000 elephants are killed each year for their tusks.

Sweet, sweet, sweet tooth

It's raining fresh and sweet today. Like real cinnamon bark. And my dog and I have an acute sugar odor and taste like *Gus*. Acute. As in yummy. Not stress like in *Gus* and other hybrids when discovered for sniffing out candies, then bound and slayed. As if the good dead had not prayed. When I prepare my mom's favorite Indian desserts with a pinch of cinnamon on a full-throated pouring day, the aroma sends my dog's nose twitching. On the stove lie containers full to the brim of *atta halwa, gajar halwa,* and *kheer.* I went overboard and cooked for a village. There was a lot of unnecessary spillage. But that's what the stomach compels. Casting bewitching spells. Wasn't sure when next it would rain like an Indian monsoon, urging me to get up and cook sweets like my mom. Inertia and desire mingle like the wagging tail of my old dog too tired to go out. We both licked our fingers. I made tea and lounged, watching the downpour. Thinking of *Gus* and viruses yet to come. My dog grumbled and lay next to me. *Sweet Tooth* was playing in the background. Too much sugar can take one down.

**Atta halwa:* wheat flour dessert

**Gajar halwa:* carrot dessert

**Kheer:* rice pudding

This poem is inspired by Gus, the 10-year-old main character in *Sweet Tooth*, a 2021 Netflix series set in a dystopian world. Gus is a hybrid of humans and deer, like many children in the movie. The hybrids are blamed for a deadly virus, H5G9.

Experimentations

Human remorse has a way of surfacing, like half-soaked, messy bits of paper in a toilet bowl. Smeared with angry words, pinching like extra rough sandpaper. You see, some movies show aliens abducting humans and on them experimenting. In real science, humans do the same to animals with specific intent. Movies may conceal subconscious fault inbuilt. Why are human fear and suffering so special? Why is separation from loved ones in humans special? Who makes humans the judge of emotional-physical relativity? Decision-makers of hidden activity in captivity in the name of alleviating diseases in humanity. Testing the last nerve of gods, angels, demons, and devils. Let's stop justifying things. Let's not drizzle our practices with blingy strings. Let's strip ourselves of artificial paramountcy cloaks. Defined seemingly by advanced, brainy strokes. Let's stop pedestalizing ourselves. Let's just call the shots and open all the cringey knots. Humans aren't predestined, precious organisms. We may throw in grandiose euphemisms. Rephrasing in ambitious rewordings. Throw around pompous aphorisms like flashy cash at wedding celebrations. And like unbelievable farts, offer explanations mired in twisted intellectual positions. But it's simple like an unseen wrinkle. Humankind needs to do a better job. Stop being their own heartthrob! And this may be one of those times, that I'll make a contract with AI for developing vaccines with no toxic trials or experimentations. Sans those damages, labeling humans as savages.

This poem is inspired by reports of extensive experimentation on animals for research purposes.

Chains

Chains are sometimes worn in gold and silver. Expensive. Shiny. Crafted and designed. Sparkly status symbols. Crooning full-throated on wrists of emperors and queens in monitored temperatures. Or humming on big stages on gilded violins. These don't rattle in cold winds. Don't rust in the rain. Don't leave dried blood stains. Except when human vs. human goes mad for possessions. In fuzzy hours can become ailing obsessions. These chains are caressed and loved and sheltered and envied. Not like chains around dogs tied outside, alone, neglected, robbing dignity like an untamed, belligerent sepsis lesion that hustles between human offenses. Cheap, thick chains that oxidize. Erode. Twisting and twisting around a neck like a wet cloth turned and squeezed numerous times to pull out the water but dried up before flattening in the scorching sunlight. What is the heart if the heart can't feel? Just mechanically clunking in the core of a junkyard's brain like a forgotten great-great-great-grandfather clock aching to tick-tock again.

This poem is inspired by the way many dogs are chained outside homes in winter, rain, or summer.

Singing flowers and whales

Slaloming along coastlines. Growing into and from biomes of waters, greens, and voices. Of grooming, mating, losing, and dying. Singing whales skirting the migratory lanes, day or nightfall, seeking partners, even for a few moments. Bliss of these unions releasing ancient *Akashic* wisdoms. Best held in the palms of their pods. Offering fragrances of completeness from one to another if chance portends. Fins not flapping, just slow dancing. No spotlights shone, just some evening whispers from afar. Just some inaudible clicks, whistles, and pulsed calls of whales that impregnate muted missives in deep oceans. Messages that your polluted sounds stifle and drown. Blaring horns, chugging fumes, propellers chopping, engines sucking away prospects, dulling trails of strings from unheard whale music. Lost desires. Lost SOS whimpers. Lost freshness of the breaths of the dying young.

**Akashic record:* Ancient records holding knowledge of all events, thoughts, words, and emotions. Scientific evidence has not revealed the actual existence of these records.

This poem is inspired by reports that life-giving and sustaining sounds, like the singing of whales, are becoming dim for other whales to pick up due to high oceanic traffic.

Survival of the fittest or sheer inconvenience

Sometimes, we might kill a small snake or squash a small fly, or a small mosquito, a small bee, a small cockroach, or a small spider. No sugar coating with sweet cider. See, I used the word small, again and again. And because they are small, humans become gutsy without sentiment. Like hidden insults spoken under a breath. Or anonymous bullying over the internet. This is a predicament. Like powerful business giants terminating small people's jobs that are hurdles to the quick speed of the evergreen gold-leaf ages. To justify they use complicated jargon, ending with a month's wages. Not even hiring a downsizer like in *Up in the Air*. As I said, no sugar coating with sweet cider, just a quick deal squaring. And on small nonhumans, our hands, feet, or a slipper, or a rolled newspaper, or a shoe suffices. Our armaments, our resources, the biggest war tool, creating our very own cesspool. Bigger animals do the same, but without thinking. Some relatives and friends, too, can be squashed in an apocalyptic Ferris wheel. Sometimes, if inclined, we might let the small insects go. Try to drive them out. Or away. Feral, feral flattening, hammering, champing, biting, feeding. It's an inconvenient kind of survival.

**Up in the Air* is a 2019 movie starring George Clooney in which he travels around the country to lay off people.

Zoos

We too live in zoos. In many zoos, like *Matryoshka* dolls, tightly stacked and confined. The universe, the Milky Way, the Earth, continents, countries, cities, homes, rooms. Some are compassionate in their zoos, some not. The yin and the yang are supposed to be a whole for the greater good. Until in tectonic plates, stubborn cracks stealthily brood. Until GMOs are couched on a tiny label. A couple of times, I've been to a zoo. Appeared enchanting, intriguing when I was young. An entrapment, confinement, it seemed when I took my son. Age and philosophical doubts chiseled away like a sculptor's sturdy hammer. I was not in awe anymore. Not enthralled anymore. Did not exclaim much. Felt with destiny a kind of a munch. Did not wish to stay long. Did not have on my lips a merry song. My feet wanted to exit; my son's hand pulled me to stay. He asked if they were happy. I said happiness is temporary, and only a child is true happiness. I held him close, as did the monkey its, and other animal moms. We all watched each other. Some cages were quiet. Some echoed calls from unseen within. Some alone humans were outside, making odd faces and jeering. My son watched them too. So did the animals through their view. After some eye-locking, the animals were the first to walk away.

**Matryoshka dolls:* A Russian set of eight nesting tea dolls

Unpartnered relics

Not all relics are found. Or studied. Or paired. Some just lay buried. Under dirt, stone, or in cupboards left behind. Or remain unpolished like uncertain roads of some choices. Or be like finished roads that disappear in the shifting of desert sands or high tides. And so, the tale appears full to some, semi to some, like *roti*, half soaked, half fresh. Or it creaks like crepitus bones in my former home. Time seems compressed like a rolled-up, empty, cracking garden water pipe without the moist hype. Or like an old newspaper browning at the bends. Everything exactly where I'd left it. Mummified in place. Morphed into an unknown space. Seemed I was viewing through a telescope. Pitch dark with a few lighted spots that didn't want to be scoped. Or they'd have sniveled, telling tales of how, after my undesired departure, they'd coped. My clothes hung straight, without expression, like soldiers at attention or little kids in many *Casablancas*. Some lay neatly folded, still in color-coded piles. Some had dropped their hue, some had permanent creases, some lay crumpled, unwashed. Some humans do not partner for life. Some animals do. Some humans demand more, rebuke more, ridicule more, exploit more, cheat more, lose more. Like moss is more slippery than rain-wet floor. Some waves never reach the shore. There is no respite. Like the sunken Titanic, unredeemable, never to see daylight. Like the starving sighs of a dim mist hovering above the eelgrass, hoping to be thicker. Like my hanger-hung clothes heave without a body. Like the silence of a solitary body in a *smadhi*. Paired animals partner up for life.

Roti: A round flatbread originating from South Asia

Crepitus: The creaking of bones with the decline of cartilage due to aging

Casablanca: A poem first published in 1826 and written by British poetess Felicia Dorothea Hemans

Smadhi: Hindi word for achieving highest meditation or a grave

The story of the endangered Himalayan respect

My respect is tall, loyal, and consistent, like my exhalations that labor hard and stand beside me to tell my tales woven in real time from a maturing, heat-cold-tested yarn. Pensive and curious like the quizzing eyes of a newborn, my respect was birthed from the centuries-long and silent shifting, splitting of the Pangea. My respect dies each time the calls of impertinency ring my way, that bear witness and testimony to the non-biogradable garbage left behind; to the animal and flora-fauna that has been altered by steps insistent on climbing me, again and again and again. No wooden mounds of the dead lie burning, though. No Vedic chants can be heard from long-bearded *sadhus,* though. Sometimes you may feel the cordiality of my deference; its ecstatic joy, like a passionate first kiss. Sometimes you may feel the chilly wound of my respect, like numbed blisters or frostbites under shoeless, sockless feet. My respect is carried on the backs of the dwindling numbers of snow leopards, musk deer, black bears, the yaks—the untamable—and all others who remain to tell the narrative of my slowly curving, painful aging back. It's my account. I just need to remember to straighten my spine.

Sadhus: A religious ascetic or holy person in Hinduism or Jainism

The Kongo *Nkisi Nkondi* and the riding dog

Incessant, loud knocking was heard. Was that a woodpecker or another bird? Seemed to come from the main door. Louder than an oil bore. It was the dilemmata who'd come calling. Like visitors who come too early, too often, and overstay. Behind them stood an army of *Nkisi* on their sturdy dogs. Behind them stood Gods and Goddesses on their vehicles—lions, horses, camels, peacocks, serpents, bulls, dragons, mice, and more. All standing with purpose, resolve, a mission. Out to rectify, destroy evil, gesturing me to polish my encasing with coconut oil and not let my anxieties boil. Oh, they were here to ease the strain! *Are there enough of you? The world's breaking down . . . we need you . . .* I shouted as they rode away into the orange sun, over the backyard fences with ancient sacred medicines and divine protections dangling from blades and knives tied to their bodies. Our wrongs crucified in them, like in Jesus. Their spiritual mirrors splintering. Each reflection whispering, chiding. Oh, how do we cover humanity's ignominy! For one final, quick moment, they all turned around. Keen-eyed. Cautious. I heard a message from their souls thrice. *Roll the dice. Roll the dice. Hey girl, roll the dice. Let not go of remaining pieces of smiles, kisses, touches, and recollections.* Oh, their magical refrain!

This poem is inspired by the Nkisi power figures found in Kongo, Africa. These figures could be human or animal and are meant to ward off evil and protect the vulnerable.

Sadism

Why have a pet dog if hitting, throwing, pummeling, are all that you know? All that you do. Your learning is limited. Your brain's minimality is exhibited. Your heart's capacity is inhibited. It seems like there are no distinct organs inside to guide you. It seems your thoughts are undeveloped. Your emotions are self-pivoted. The limping legs, the resounding destitute yaps, the worn-out watery eyes, the dry mouths, their wilting stomachs, their lackluster skin, their sickness—nothing impacts you. Couldn't you instead go buy a punching bag for your issues? Or use pillows? No bathing with soap and water of your senses? No putting your behavior through a wash cycle? No holding your hand before thrashing? No kicking your own foot before lashing? No tears roll down your cheeks later. No confessions follow. Neither does your spit feel any lumps in your throat when you swallow, jumping instead like red hot chilies on a rouged tongue long after midnight.

A bear on 395

395 is only a numerical example. Happens more often than not. On speeding highways that appear as sleeping giants whose whiskers, if tingled too much, will yawn and gobble. Gobble. Gobble, leaving humans and cars tangled and mangled. And on those very wide, dug-out, flattened, tarred, marked roads, sometimes animals big and small wander. Wander and wonder. Helpless, confused by human and automated sounds, running helter-skelter through zipping traffic, over the median, over the rails, back onto the rapid lanes, flabbergasted by spatial muddle. In one video the bear seemed young. Out to find a mate and make its own den. Inexperienced in the ways of metal and speed. The police were called. Drivers slowed but none created a barrier shielding the bear. Only more videos were posted with eye-grabbing headlines. Their homes encroached. Homelands poached. And sometimes gobbled on fortified roads. No compensation for their families. They aren't "sentient" enough to grasp the shrinking of their species. And then the evening news writes off a bear hit and run on 395 as a minimal deficit from which we can easily recover. Like missing the morning news.

This poem is inspired by a true story of a bear killed on highway 395.

Circus of life

Up and down and all around
No need for the sneer or the frown
Lock your eyes with my hand
See the leash leaping to the band
See the people laugh and exclaim
With mouths wide open at your fame
I'll throw you glazed pretty morsels
If you'll act obedient for the paying mortals.

It's really the modern age. I mean modern, modern. We can even call it beyond post-modern. I mean AI are almost our companions. Like a body not at ease initially, skeptically trying new yogic poses, circuses can still entertain without hints of the unknown, the peculiar, or the unnecessary awe. Without animals. Without the atypical. Without "sentient" ignorance being a reasonable drink. Recollections of the so-called glorious, manifested destiny kinda former entertainment roll by like snow globes hurrying across summer fields. Mega tents lie in tattering heaps along with aging, grumbling ropes infested with ants and dried horse dung. There are just a few circuses left now with tuneless songs blaring from burnished mikes. Folks are smartening up. There is no victory in shocking, whipping animals to perform. There is no victory in claps echoing only in your head. There is no victory if the places are swapped. Choice is not a luxury after all.

Angoras, downs, alligators, snakes, cows, buffalos, rabbits, sheep, ostriches, etc., etc., etc.

Please stop. Stop my fingers from typing countless etc., etc., etc. It's like a constant buzzing of the bees. They won't stop. Why should they when they are trying to tell me something. But what would I repeat that the world doesn't already know? And ignore. Cupboards of some are full of affluent, not-required artifacts. These are just the facts. Powder-sugar supple angoras, or rare furs, stand firm, though I can see their shoulders drooping. Eyes at the tip of the droop are vacant and tear-layered. Like untoasted bread, thickly larded. Or a shaped-to-taste piece of meat that hangs with straps swinging like bells in an empty, burnt church. And then the winter sleep for some is surrounded by the fluff of down feathers angrily plucked, jerked. What if it were a handful of hair from a human head? Some parade another's skin on theirs. Not the kind that two people display in lovemaking. But one of nightmares of animals minding their own business, surrounded and exterminated. Like in the middle of the night, people on unlit streets are spilled. Like slaves pulled from families never to know a dear one's hug. And then, on two straight legs, walk rigidly the self-righteous. I feel the tainted heat, the needless soreness, the shame that comes from watching pure eyes, partially alive in frames poked and skinned, looking here and there on a thick, round wooden block or on the cold, coarse floor.

This poem is inspired by the use of animal products in the fashion industry.

Bullfight

I went to a bullfight once. Parents took us siblings. Thrusting info from newspaper clippings. During the fight, they became converts, embarrassed by their patronization of a chilly game. It seemed like judgment day in court for a crime not done but simply as bulls to be born. And then for their organs to be gouged and torn. I cried for the outnumbered bulls and the collective mob passion. Ready for their soiling and the bulls' toiling. Like bubbles boiling in water, impatient to spill over. No time for a makeover. And the matadors, resplendent in scarlet and black, stood with a convexed back. Similar to that of a bull just before the last sword enters its robust body. Resistance, counterattacks, running around in trapped circles are useless. When a shining title drives intent and emotion, it is pointless. With slick conniving, the unsuspecting mighty fall. Atop the *monteras* flying, I could see the piercing oculus of the bulls' sailplaning.

**Monteras:* Plural for montera, a matador's hat

Blood bank

I live in this narrow kennel where the enflamed is all over. My waste and my blood appear the same to me. And being here is neither accidental nor gentle. It's deprived of even a basic cloth. And stale is my food broth. Where do I lay my jutting bones? How do I eat the same soggy kibble, day in and day out? No sustenance variety. No petting, no chin scratching. Would you be part of such a sick fraternity? The cold of the kennel cage slashes my body wide open with gashes. I don't see the outside world much. Nor feel the air on my rotting skin declutch. My teeth are yellow, my body exhausted. Remembrances don't give me company nor nudge any yearning. Nor do I wag my tail. Nor do the cats here purr a lively sound. All decency is drowned. Everything is a set-up, mired, weird, and wired. This is where I and my fellow mates are punctured with needles frequently. Without aftercare. Like you'd not like to be after communal surgery in an infected amphitheater. They say our blood will help others of our kind. Those who live in homes with love. Do humans who donate blood live alone in cages till they die? Bonded blood for the free.

This poem is inspired by reports that tell us about unclean dog and cat blood banks which are very inhospitable places.

Nameless stray dogs

In some places, nameless strays roam the streets. For food, pats, warmth. On those muddled streets as winds slice their howls; their needs they foreclose like homes with unpaid loans. I see, I see that many named humans come through in heavy boots, and the dogs' lives, they chew, coil, and spit like juice-less betelnut leaves. Their tender eyes, their fear they don't see, instead kicking them in their belly as they poop and pee. Sentients become worse than so-called non-sentients as strays are hunted by the sober and the heartless inebriant. The elected have bailed, nailed, sailed, failed as they dance bizarrely in an everyday revolving ball. Who leads the brawl is your call. I sit in the muddy rain, pull my dripping heart out, stare at it with tears now ebbing in a tight drought. Then I try pulling out my dried, sticky, dense tears as they sit on haunches in their gluey, colorless hue. Only nameless strays come lick my wounds on those befuddled streets.

Leaving me

At a traffic light at a busy intersection in a big city is not cool. The milling-spilling of the crowds, their blankness, their antipathy, their timidity gave you courage. Between you, your actions, your emotions, there was an unholy marriage. You tossed me like an unknown rock into a hurrying river so I would get lost. Or hurt. Nothing left to build. I was just a toy for temporary amusement, so you threw me away like half-eaten, cold, stale food, like old stuff unworthy of even donation. Sounding our bond's castration. Until the light turned green, and others honked, I kept jumping up to the window, thinking you were just playing a game. Like, follow your commands and get a treat, kind. I whined and pined. Your long arm through the window kept pushing me back onto the road. I thought it was a jestful code. I thought it was still a game, yay, but what an outrage when the lights opened your journey and mine remained fixed at that intersection to decay. I jumped faster and higher and ran behind your car. The engine and your sprinting took you away, bidding me an indecent goodbye. Hey, come back; this game is not fun anymore.

This poem is inspired by numerous accounts about people opening their windows or doors at traffic lights and leaving their pet dogs or abandoning them on city streets or outskirts.

Ride me if you must

You may ride me and feel splendid. You may place your weight on me and feel rested. And smarter from the thronal elevation on another body. Your aching feet, cramping legs, fright, or lethargy prevent you from walking. Your two are inadequate, so you use my in-compliance four. Give it up! Or give me up! History or culture will not vilify you. Up and down the hill we go; your feet are up, mine are rough. Ropes, stirrups, saddles aren't my friends by any stretch. And my scars, grazes are my badges of honor that I try to cover. At times, I feel nauseated when you park me in the hot sun without satiating my basic needs. Thirst. Food. Basic. I won't snatch yours; I'll do with just hay and straw. Butterflies try to flutter around, drying the sweat on my forehead. One or two, I could swear, blew me a flying kiss. Yet I see only the dark hole into which I can fall if the ground beneath, I miss. You will walk away like folks who have sex without emotions. And I'll continue to be ridden by countless souls satiating their desire or thrills to climb a mountain, pay abeyance, or enjoy a setting sun. Give it up or give me up! Moss and the sun have changed me. My legs are green, my paws yellow, and the blue on top is you. Enjoying this thrill while my sanity is splitting at its core.

This poem is inspired by the use of donkeys, in many parts of the world, to carry people up and down mountain pathways to cultural, historical, or religious sites.

About the Author

Dr. Anita Nahal is an educator and writer. She has worked in higher education, both in teaching and administration, at various universities for over thirty years. She's been a Fulbright scholar and an NEH fellowship awardee among other laurels in her academic career. She has published, presented papers and seminars, and created numerous workshops in her discipline of history. She teaches at a university in Washington D.C.

On the creative side, Anita is a poet, flash fictionist, children's book writer, a recent novelist, and even more recent short film maker. A two-time Pushcart Prize-nominated Indian American author, she won the Nissim Prize for Excellence in Literature for her poetry-prose novel, *drenched thoughts* (Authorspress, 2023) in 2024.

Anita was a finalist for the Tagore Literary Prize in 2023 for her fourth ekphrastic prose poetry collection, *Kisses at the espresso bar* (Kelsay Books, 2022). Her third prose poetry collection, *What's wrong with us Kali women?* (Kelsay Books, 2021), was nominated by Cyril Dabydeen, poet laureate emeritus, Ottawa, Canada, as the best poetry book of 2021, for British *Ars Notoria*. It is mandatory reading in a multicultural society course at Utrecht University, the Netherlands.

Anita has one novel, four poetry collections, one of flash fiction, four books for children, and five edited anthologies published. Anita's poems have appeared in numerous journals in the US, UK, Asia, and Australia and anthologized in many collections, including *The Polaris Trilogy* (2024), *The Best Asian Poetry* (2021–22), *Yearbook of Indian Poetry in English* (2021), and *Twenty Contemporary Indian English Poets* (2024), the latter released by India's Academy of Letters—the Sahitya Akademi.

Her poems are also housed at Stanford University's Digital Humanities Initiative. One of her poems, "Hold on baby, we'll soon be home," was included as part of a video produced by Doordarshan TV, Kolkata, India. Some of Anita's poems are part of an online collection of poetry and art, *Crossarts-In Between The Lines* on Canadian and Indian diaspora women writers. And one of her poems has also been delivered on the moon as part of *The Polaris Trilogy*.

Recently, Anita ventured into short filmmaking on her poems, and her first short, "Clubs my sinful dance muse," was awarded the Best Super Short Film Award by the Five Continents International Film Festival, Venezuela (2024). It was also screened at the Alibag and Goa Short Film Festivals in India in 2024.

Anita is the secretary of the Montgomery Chapter, Maryland Writers Association, and former editor of the newsletter for Poetry Society of Virginia. She is also an active member of the Northern Virginia Writers Club and the Poetry Society of Virginia.

Anita is the daughter of Sahitya Akademi; award-winning Indian novelist and professor, Late Dr. Chaman Nahal; and educationist Late Dr. Sudarshna Nahal. Her family incudes her son, daughter-in-law, a grandson, and a golden doodle gal.

More on her at:
anitanahal.com

www.ingramcontent.com/pod-product-compliance
Lightning Source LLC
Chambersburg PA
CBHW071013160426
43193CB00012B/2031